T0113502

BELOW-ZERO
NURSING

DR. J. GRACE EVES DNP, RN

WESTBOW
PRESS®
A DIVISION OF THOMAS NELSON
& ZONDERVAN

Scripture taken from the New King James Version®. Copyright © 1982 by Thomas Nelson. Used by permission. All rights reserved.

This book is a work of non-fiction. Unless otherwise noted, the author and the publisher make no explicit guarantees as to the accuracy of the information contained in this book and in some cases, names of people and places have been altered to protect their privacy.

WestBow Press books may be ordered through booksellers or by contacting:

WestBow Press
A Division of Thomas Nelson & Zondervan
1663 Liberty Drive
Bloomington, IN 47403
www.westbowpress.com
1 (866) 928-1240

Because of the dynamic nature of the Internet, any web addresses or links contained in this book may have changed since publication and may no longer be valid. The views expressed in this work are solely those of the author and do not necessarily reflect the views of the publisher, and the publisher hereby disclaims any responsibility for them.

Any people depicted in stock imagery provided by Thinkstock are models, and such images are being used for illustrative purposes only. Certain stock imagery © Thinkstock.

ISBN: 978-1-9736-0883-7 (sc)
ISBN: 978-1-9736-0884-4 (hc)
ISBN: 978-1-9736-1246-9 (e)

Library of Congress Control Number: 2017918064

Print information available on the last page.

WestBow Press rev. date: 12/22/2017

To my husband, John, who helped my dream come true. Also, to my sons Eric and Isaac who support me in my nursing career and are a part of my many adventures-which continue to shape their lives.

CONTENTS

PREFACE

When I began to write this book, I couldn't help but think about the history of nursing and all it meant to me as a young nurse. As I began to write down some of my memories and observations during my time nursing in the Arctic, I noticed how the philosophy of Florence Nightingale rings true, more than a hundred years after she lived. I didn't know how much I would be called upon to embrace Florence Nightingale's goal of nursing: to provide a safe and caring environment mixed with effective observation to stimulate an individual's health and well-being. As I looked back at my nursing career, I noticed a trend, that I too have had that same goal for my nursing career.

So I thought I would write a book, in a story-type format, that would give you a taste of my experiences in Hay River, Northwest Territories, Canada. These experiences and adventures have continued to guide my family's life and my nursing career.

Even upon arriving in Hay River I was immediately aware of the Dene Tribe's (First Nation people) wisdom and connection to the environment. Their focus was always on order and balance while emphasizing how everything is sacred even down to their everyday life. This all-inclusive view of the world as a balance between nature, the animal kingdom, and humans taught me to think beyond my own life and experiences. I started to see Florence Nightingale's philosophy come to life—that is, the importance of one's environment— even more than it ever had before.

I learned quite a bit from the Dene Tribe, most notably not to accumulate too much "stuff" in life but to respect another culture that is so different from my own. Respect is key to getting along with anyone who isn't like us, especially if we are to live among other cultures and share their "turf" (or in my case, their tundra). I also learned how it isn't a person's title that defines the person but rather character.

This opportunity gave me insight into the importance of knowing and understanding cultures. Nursing in Hay River was all about customizing care to fit with the First Nation and Inuit people's cultural values, beliefs, traditions, practices, and lifestyle. I learned how successful nursing care could only occur within the individual's cultural context.

Hay River is a place of extremes. We were isolated from society yet I felt as if I had no privacy. There was an abundance of nature all around us but lack of the modern environment and outlook on life. The temperature was brutally cold in the winter yet the summers had twenty-four hour sunlight and were bug-ridden.

But Hay River forever influenced my life and my journey as a Registered Nurse.

My family and I left Hay River, the northern wilderness, in 1991. In all honesty, it was the longest two years of our lives. Yet, how many people experience the beautiful landscape of northern Canada? How many people get THAT CLOSE to the North Pole? And how many people experience the enriching culture of the Dene Tribe? I thank God I got to fulfill the dream I had been called to—serving and caring for the First Nation people of the Northwest Territories.

One scripture comes to mind that sums up my experiences so well: "love your neighbor as yourself." It is a commandment found in the Old Testament (Leviticus 19:18) and New Testament (Mark 12:31), teaching us to show our neighbors the love of Christ no matter our differences.

CHAPTER 1

THE DREAM

Delight yourself also in the Lord, And He shall give you the desires of your heart.

(Psalm 37: 4)

As we boarded the plane for Hay River, I felt the joy and exuberance of a lifelong dream about to come true... well... as much as my mid-thirty-something years constituted "lifelong." I just knew I had been groomed for this adventure since the day I was born. I couldn't wait to experience the future that was ahead of me.

Both my mother and grandfather had worked among the First Nation people. Stories of them had filled my childhood-about how my ancestors had already forged a reputation among the First Nation people that would no doubt make it easier for me to serve among them once they knew more about the history of my family.

My grandfather had worked at a local pulp and paper mill in Pine Falls, Manitoba. He measured the wood the First Nation people brought into the mill and paid them money in accordance with the amount of wood he received. Since he was honest about the amount of wood coming in, the First Nation people lined up for him to measure their wood. They knew he would not shortchange them as so many others had before.

His daughter (my mother) worked in a food store when she was a teenager. She carried on the tradition of honesty and integrity that my grandfather taught her, by his example. Throughout her time at the food store, she refused to give the First Nation people spoiled food as her supervisor had instructed her to do. Instead, she gave them the full amount of food they had paid for. It was as fresh as anyone else would have received.

My grandfather's good reputation among the First Nation people was never more aptly illustrated than when they quite unexpectedly returned my grandfather's kindness to them. There came a time when my grandfather was sick and unable to work, so he wasn't getting paid. He had no wood or food for the family. Somehow the First Nation people knew about our family's difficulty and delivered food and wood to my grandparents' doorstep continually until my grandfather was able to return to work. They were the only people in the entire town who helped my grandparents.

My father was liked as well. I still remember him taking our family back to Manitoba. It had been about 30 years since he last visited. When we arrived at Pine Falls, my father insisted we visit the First Nation people's reservation. He wanted us to get a taste of their culture and lifestyle. So we got into my uncle's car, and he drove us to the reservation.

We pulled up to their local corner store and saw a crowd of elderly First Nation people standing around, smoking. My dad opened the car door, and before he could even get out of the car, the men were at the door shaking his hand and welcoming him back. The older generation of First Nation people had apparently remembered the good relationship they shared with our family.

I was about to become the next significant contributor to a generations-long family legacy of working among the First Nation people. I still remember that nurse who gave a talk about her experiences on a reservation in Northern Ontario, and that's when I knew I wanted to nurse among the First Nation people, too. Her stories captured my attention. She described the beauty and mystery of working among the First Nation people. It was as if this way of life was not transformed by the influence of the modern day. Rather she indicated that it barely changed at all.

I remember the day I shared my calling with my husband, John. It was before we got married. He simply said, "We'll work it out." He had a successful flooring business he would need to give up before we could go.

As time passed my firstborn son, Eric, turned four. I realized that my dream of practicing nursing among the First Nation people was fading further into the back of my mind. I knew if we didn't make a move at that point, we would probably never go.

Many of the senior patients I cared for at the time were telling me the same thing. "You need to fulfill your dreams while you're still young," they would tell me. "Otherwise you'll never go."

Although my mom and dad always said to live life, up to that point, I'd lived the same kind of life everyone else in the world was living. I'd attended school, found a job, and had a family. Now, I was about to uproot my family in pursuit of my dream.

The day soon came when the movers pulled up and packed our things. It was September 1989.

* * *

We had already taken flight by the time I awoke from the haze of my daydream recollections. The sound of my four-year-old son sniffling back tears in the seat next to me had jarred me out of my blissful state. Eric had just left his beloved pet bunny behind. I put my arm around him to comfort him, trying to pass along the same assurance I had that this change would be the best thing that could ever happen to our family.

I reached underneath the seat in front of me and pulled out my purse. I took out a picture of a First Nation doll that I had gotten for Christmas when I was a little girl. She had dark skin and wore a parka with fur around the hood. I put it in front of Eric, and he seemed fascinated by the picture of me as a little girl dearly holding this doll. I tried to explain to him how where we were going we would meet people who wore this type of winter coat. He was fascinated with the fur and how the parka had no buttons. I said to him that we would try to get him a parka similar to that one. Eric leaned over, put his head in my lap, and fell asleep.

A minute or so later, I laid my head back against the headrest and dozed off to sleep.

CHAPTER 2

THE REALITY

In everything give thanks; for this is the will of God in Christ Jesus for you.

(1 Thessalonians 5:18)

Turbulence jarred me awake, and I looked out the window to see where we were. All I could see was nothingness... wilderness... just wilderness. If the earth were flat, this would have been its edge. My heart sank as my mind and heart realized that this place was truly one of the last wilderness areas in North America.

For the first time, I realized how far we really were from family and friends, how isolated we were. I was overwhelmingly homesick. I was overpowered with the realization that we were now in the subarctic wilderness, a land I had never known.

What in the world have I done? I asked myself.

All those sacrifices I'd asked my family to make for me to get here.

How could I have not seen this coming? Nearly my entire family has lived in Canada. I was raised on stories about the First Nation people. I guess I had just imagined I would be feeling different about where we were going. How could I have been so wrong?

All I could do at that point was rely on the Lord Jesus Christ for comfort and pray that my family would not be angry with me for bringing them to Hay River. Jesus promises us in Matthew 11:28-29 that He will give rest to those who "labor and are heavy laden." He tells us to take His yoke upon us and learn from Him because He is "gentle and lowly in heart" and we will find rest for our souls.

I needed that rest, not the physical rest that comes from being tired, but the spiritual rest that comes from knowing that the LORD is with me and that He will make my life here better than it looked when we first arrived, closer (much closer) to the dream I had envisioned. So I prayed unendingly for months until I felt the peace that passes all understanding.

We touched down and waited for the plane to stop and for the flight attendants to give us clearance to "deplane." Of course, everyone jumped out of their seats at once, all trying to reclaim their carry-ons from the overhead compartments. Everyone was so tightly jammed in that plane, John and I waited until some of the passengers in front of us began walking forward with their baggage before we even attempted to get up.

After we successfully retrieved our bags, John, Eric, and I joined the line to the front of the plane. I was the first to reach the entrance of the plane; an arctic blast of painfully cold wind pummeled my face. I stood there for a moment almost reluctant to take the first step towards our new life. Before I started down the stairs, I reached back quickly to make sure Eric was securely bundled up and pulled his scarf up over his nose and mouth.

"What's the matter?" John asked.

"Make sure you're covered up. It's bitter cold up here."

We had never felt that level of cold, beyond anything we had ever experienced.

We entered the tiny airport and waited for our checked luggage. My sense of dread had grown even more overwhelming since the reality of subarctic air had hit me. I prayed for the peace of God once again.

After we retrieved our baggage, we entered a taxi to take us to a motel. The taxi looked as if a rabid animal had gone through it. The seat was full of holes and visible springs from the cushions. That's what we sat on all the way to the motel, which unfortunately didn't look much better than the cab. It certainly didn't smell any better.

The outside of the motel was made of logs that looked like they'd been eaten by termites, as if a termite could live in this weather. When we walked into the front of this motel, the place wreaked of alcohol, tobacco, and urine, as if a hundred dogs had peed on the carpet. I kept wondering if the motel even had a cleaning staff, or if that smell was normal up here.

We left immediately. There was no way I could let Eric spend even one minute in one of their rooms, much less an entire night. So we got back out in the frigid cold, got back into the animal-eaten taxi, and went to the only other motel in town. Thankfully, the motel and our room were much cleaner.

We arrived at the motel around dinner time. As we were unpacking, I thought back to growing up in Canada's universal health care system where the focus is all about the environment.

The Canadian government started universal health care in the 1950's to reduce the number of premature deaths. Premature death was defined as anyone who died before they reached their 70th birthday. By the 1970's they were amazed that people were still dying prematurely, that is before turning 70. The Canadian government looked deeper into this finding and discovered the reason. It was because an individual's lifestyle and the environment they lived in had more to do with a person's health than the health care system.

I realized the environment we were now living in was very different than the one we left. All I could think about was what Florence Nightingale had emphasized in her writings-the environment is key to one's health and well-being.

After unpacking, we proceeded to one of the only restaurants in town and ordered the whitefish. Our server, a young man, perhaps the son of the owner, brought us the most beautiful plate of fish, and set it in the center of the table. He brought Eric a bison burger. John and I cut off a helping of the fish as the server began to tell us stories about the flood that happened in 1963.

He talked to us as if time was divided between before the flood and after the flood. Apparently, the annual spring break-up seemed to create anxiety in the town. In 1963, a force of water built up behind a twelve-mile-long ice jam just above Hay River. When the ice jam exploded, the deep, flash flooding hit the town. Everything was under 3 feet of water or had been swept away. It only took minutes for all this to happen. Every year the town set up a twenty-four-hour watch so everyone could be alerted if anything similar would occur. Although spring was months away, the people of the town were already talking about it and preparing for the twenty-four-hour watch.

The server was really quite talkative and informative. As we were preparing to dig into our meals, he brought us a dish of bannock, a round grain bread that looked much like a pie. We each cut a piece of it. Later we found out that this was the kind of bread they baked. We enjoyed our meal thoroughly and retired to our room for the evening.

The next morning, I got up early and cooked some oatmeal I brought from home. Our motel room had a hot plate and small refrigerator. The evening before we had stopped at the only corner store for some milk. Our breakfast was simple but hot and satisfying.

I was, however, thinking about the breakfast we ate before leaving our home, St. Catharines Ontario, Canada. We had enjoyed a breakfast buffet with such delicacies as blueberry and walnut pancakes, Canadian bacon, Quiche Lorraine, and breakfast pizza. It would be awhile before we would be able to enjoy fresh blueberries, the taste of Quiche Lorraine, and breakfast pizza.

We finished eating breakfast and headed to the cab we'd called for an hour or so earlier when the manager stopped us for a quick chat.

"I hear you're going to get a car and look for a place to stay today."

I looked at John and said, "Did we mention that when we checked in yesterday?"

John just shrugged. "Must have."

"We were so tired last night," I said. "Who knows what we said?"

I looked at the manager and nodded. "Yes we are," said John.

"Well, your cab driver will know where the only dealership is," began the manager, "and as far as housing, there's a neighborhood just before the river ice road..."

I interrupted, "The river ice road. Will we have to drive on that ice road?"

"Yes. It is actually the frozen river...well, an ice road. Don't worry; it's safe to drive over..... Anyway," he resumed, "once you get your car, there are some nice homes for rent nearby. Some are houses and some are mobile homes. The houses are near the row of spruce trees over that way; it's where a bear was shot last year."

"Bears?" I said, suddenly a little frightened.

"We get them every now and then. You won't be able to get a license for hunting (Big Game) for at least two years. I'd strongly suggest you get to know how to survive here in the north."

"Thank you."

"OK, then, take care, folks. Welcome to Hay River."

"Thanks," said John.

We got into the taxi and instructed the driver to take us to the dealership first. Once the cab dropped us off, a salesman approached us to help us find the vehicle we needed.

We decided to look for a car since John's work truck, which was being transported up here, would be arriving soon. We had the truck transported up here so we could haul anything we might need.

We were in the north Canadian wilderness, so houses and business establishments were spread out over the entire well-snowed, iced area. There was nothing else around except trees along the tree line, though many looked more like shrubs than trees. There were probably animals in the area, too; we just hadn't seen any yet.

We noticed a green Ford that would work perfectly for us to get around. We would have John's truck for the snowy and icy conditions. It's truck bed could be used for hauling food and other things we would need. Plus it was well used.

Buying a car really started to give us a sense of how things worked up here. There was no such thing as negotiation. You see there was just one dealership and one mechanic shop. Both owned by the same family.

After we purchased the car and before we drove off, the salesman said, "I understand you're looking for a home to rent."

"Now I know we didn't tell him that," I mumbled to John.

"You'll start seeing some homes a mile or so down the river," said the salesman, "where the line of spruce trees is; that's where the bear was shot."

We've heard this before, I thought. "OK, thank you so much."

I thought back to this experience a lot during the next two years. It seemed that people knew our business, even before we knew it. This was very evident not only when we were looking for a place to live, but also when John brought home our first dog, Sheba, a couple of weeks after we arrived.

There are no pet stores up there, so John went to the place where they hold the dogs who are picked up. If a pack of dogs came into town, the town officials would shoot them because they would form packs that would quickly become a danger to the public. If there was just one stray dog, they would only hold the dog for a couple of days. We actually became known as the family who would take in any stray dog because we didn't like to see the animals shot. Plus, there were no vets to treat injured dogs. Although, often the town doctor would administer care to the pets in town and fix broken legs-right in the hospital.

John went to the holding place and picked up a sweet German Shepard mix. We believed she was part fox. Sheba was beautiful. I was just returning to the hospital from a visit to the reservation and found out about Sheba when one of the maintenance workers asked me about our new dog.

I said to him, "We don't have a dog."

He responded by telling me he not only saw John walking down the street with a dog but saw him building a dog house earlier that day. Sure enough, when I walked outside, I was greeted by not only John and Eric but also the new addition to our family.

People in town truly knew our business and everyone else's, even before we knew it.

CHAPTER 3

WINTER WONDERLAND

... I am with you always...

(Matthew 28:20)

We drove for what seemed like forever, not because of all the wide-open space, but because driving in the snow and ice was slow-going. We were getting our first taste of it as we drove around trying to find a place to rent.

As we drove, we came upon one house that looked…interesting. It was half built with large creates surrounding it. Apparently, houses were shipped into the north in creates and were put together similar to how Eric built his little play towns with Lego. Except there were no colors, just light brown wood.

We continued to encounter these types of homes, as well as looked at mobile homes for the next two weeks, living out of our motel, until one day we found a nice mobile home. It had a light blue exterior, so it color-coordinated well with the snow, not that we were looking for that; it's just an observation on my part.

We noticed the mobile home had a snowmobile plugged into an outlet outside. We guessed it either belonged to the landlord, or it was left by the previous tenant who, for whatever reason, either didn't want it or couldn't take it.

It was a gorgeous snowy scene that God had delivered to us. I felt that same sort of feeling when I flew to the top of the world, Tuktoyaktuk, Northwest Territories the next year. This is when I saw the life of the Inuit people (known by most as Eskimos) with all its adventures and opportunities. It was an area that was above the tree line, where the boreal forest meets the tundra.

Once we'd paid the down payment for our new place, we retrieved our luggage from our motel room, loaded it in the car, and went inside. We'd have to wait for our furniture to arrive before we could unpack. Until then, we were living out of our suitcases, somewhat appropriate for the wilderness. The next day we would arrange for the delivery of the rest of our clothing, dishes, living room and bedroom furniture.

Eric rushed down the front steps, outlined with a rugged wood railings on both sides, to play in the snow. He saw something not too far in the distance that looked like a rather large snowball and started running toward it, presumably to pick it up and throw it. But before he could even get close to it, the snowball opened its eyes and scurried off into the distance. It was an arctic fox that had been curled up in the snow until an innocent little boy scared it away.

Eric began chasing the frightened little creature, and John ran after him. We were in a new area, and in a great place for a preschooler to get lost in the snow without anything to mark the path home. John caught up with Eric, whose little legs were fortunately not fast enough to take him very far, and took his hand.

On their way back to the house, they saw some kids not too far off. Three of them were playing drums, and a couple of others looked as if they were playing a game.

"Can I go play with them?" Eric asked.

"Sure. I'll walk you over there."

After they got to where the kids were standing, John asked them if Eric could play.

"Sure," one of them said. He knelt to Eric and said, "I'm holding an object in one of my hands. Guess which one it's in."

Eric thought for a moment and looked at the other boy's fists to try to figure out which hand held the object. Eric tapped the boy's right hand, and the boy opened it up. Eric had guessed right!

After a few more guesses, John said, "Chum (that was John's nickname for Eric), we need to be getting back. It's almost time for dinner."

Dinner! John thought. We still needed to stock the fridge, or we wouldn't have anything to eat. John raced Eric back to the house.

Both ran in, and John said, "Sweetheart, we need to go to the store. We don't have anything to eat here yet, and I don't know when the store closes."

It was already dark outside, even though it was four o'clock in the afternoon. We soon found out that during the winter, it was just as dark in the middle of the day as it was in the middle of the night. Yet just as there was very little light in the winter, the sun never set in the summer. It was just as sunny at two in the morning as it was at two in the afternoon.

John took Eric by the hand once again, and all three of us ran to the truck and jumped in, the truck that had arrived earlier that day. We drove to the store as fast as we could. There was even a place to plug our truck in to keep the engine from freezing while we were shopping. We dashed in to pick up some fresh fish, vegetables, bread, and desserts-(What four-year-old doesn't love sweets, to say nothing of the adults?). Although, there was little to choose from.

As we headed back to the truck to put our groceries in the truck bed, we noticed a pack of dogs approaching. Not knowing whether they were friendly, we hurried into the truck and started driving home before they reached us.

On our way back, Eric looked out the back window and said, "Daddy! Birds are eating our food!"

John stopped the truck and got out to shoo the ravens away.

John quickly inspected the grocery bags. They hadn't had time to really sink their teeth into our food before Eric noticed them. They'd only gotten to one bag of groceries. They flew away with it.

We thought that the ravens taking groceries from the back of the truck was shocking and astounding. But as time passed we saw many situations that amazed us about the ravens, who proved their problem-solving skills and intelligence over and over again.

The only way to describe a raven is that they look like an extremely large crow. In fact, they are a hardy powerful bird that can live in minus 50 below Fahrenheit. They are bold and had such strength that they could easily pick up and fly away with a full green garbage bag. We had never witnessed anything quite like it.

One day as we were going down the street we saw a few ravens engaged in a game with a dog. The dog was tied up. We could see that there were a couple of ravens distracting the dog as a few others worked together and lifted the dog's dish in the air. They were simply amazing birds that the First Nation people had many legends about, especially regarding their intelligence, resourcefulness, and reputation for stealing food.

The ptarmigan was another common bird, seen year round. This is a game bird, related to the grouse. It's actually the "official game bird" in parts of Canada. These birds were very interesting with feathers that covered their feet. This made their feet look like snowshoes. In the summer the feathers are brown and yellow. In the winter the feathers are as white as snow. I remember eating ptarmigan at a friend's home once, though I didn't know what kind of meat it was until after dinner.

After we finally returned home with our groceries, I cooked up enough fish and vegetables for the family, served it with bread, and then we headed off to bed...on the floor. We'd brought some sleeping bags to use until our furniture arrived. Eric didn't mind. This was one big camping trip to a four-year-old boy.

As we laid on the floor in our sleeping bags, I couldn't help but notice the bright, pale green, dancing Northern Lights through the undressed windows. The darkness on that clear night made the lights appear in what seemed to be scattered clouds of light. Once in a while, I would see shooting rays that lit up the sky with an unusual glow. I watched the night sky thinking about the beauty God has given us to enjoy and how we should never forget that God is with us.

The next day would be a busy one. It would be my first day working among the Dene Tribe as a nurse, and John's first-day training to be a volunteer EMT/Firefighter. He took this training as he waited for his job at the correctional facility to start. But I couldn't stop thinking of the bear I heard about the entire time we were settling into Hay River. Do they come here often? I wondered. I hope we don't see one tonight. My heart was pounding as I thought about it.

Soon, however, concern turned into exhaustion, and I finally fell asleep. I dreamed a polar bear opened our front door and found us all asleep in the living room. He came over to Eric first and started sniffing him. I woke up screaming, "Eric!"

John awoke, but Eric was too tired to wake up. He'd had a busy day chasing that fox and playing a game with those children earlier.

"What's the matter?" John asked.

"Oh...nothing," I said as I realized it was all a dream.

I had broken out in a cold sweat, so I wiped my face and neck before lying back down. A cold sweat could be deadly in Hay River if you were outside because it could quickly turn to frostbite, a problem I would have to treat frequently as a nurse in these parts, a fact I would learn all too soon....

CHAPTER 4

EARNING RESPECT

A good name is to be chosen rather than great riches, loving favor rather than silver and gold.

(Proverbs 22:1)

L et's face it; I was the new kid on the block. The folks I would be caring for were native to this land, so I was a little nervous. John and I would need to earn the respect of these people if we were to work among them.

I had a good start, though, I thought as I drove to the hospital that morning to meet with the hospital staff, receive any advice anyone had for me, and learn my marching orders, so to speak. I would be going to the reservation that day.

I remember sitting there telling them of my family's history with the First Nation people of Manitoba, and the good reputation of my mom, dad, and grandparents.

Plus, nursing had always been a well-revered profession in Hay River since the 1890s. By the 1950s, nurses had sort of a "headquarters" in the center of town and had the reputation of giving up their beds for patients and newborns, who routinely slept in the nurse's bedroom. Nurses also carried medical bags as they responded to calls in the community. In fact, the nurses had the opportunity for professional independence that resulted in such excellent care that very few people had to be sent out of the area, such as Yellowknife, for treatment by doctors. Nurses, who ventured to this area of the world, had a sense of service, duty, and compassion which was essential to the health and wellbeing for the people of Hay River.

"As far as your duties," the Nurse Coordinator began, "most of the healthcare you will be providing will be done in the Dene homes. Watch out for frostbite; it happens very fast, and it's very common here, so you'll be doing a lot of treating for that. Be sure to check everyone you visit because they may not be able to feel if they have frostbite. It's very dangerous. It can go all the way to the bone to the point that it looks like the skin is eroding away."

"Also look for scabies and lice. These may be apparent if you see someone scratching incessantly or if you see eggs in their hair or something crawling over the clothing. We have common laundry areas here where you'll bring affected clothes to wash them."

"What you will find is that the Inuit people are careful not to talk much. In fact, they only talk when they need to-more inclined to listen and observe then speak. They say we talk too much and will have to answer for all our rhetoric when we get to heaven."

"You'll also be responsible for arranging for meals to be taken to their homes, and organizing classes and seminars for the other nurses to keep them up-to-date on the latest medical information. In fact, we have a gerontology doctor who comes about once a year. His visit this year starts tomorrow actually. You will have to pick him up when the plane arrives tomorrow. I know the nurse before you would arrange a class for the nurses so he could provide up-to-date information on caring for our seniors."

I was also warned about the weather.

The Nursing Coordinator said, "There will be times that if you are out in the cold with your skin exposed for more than a few seconds, you will get frostbite."

She also talked about the ice river road. "Cross the river with our van (the Northwest Territory government provided a van for the Home Care nursing staff for medical treatments, meal delivery, and transportation). The ice is thick, a bit slippery but safe to drive over."

"Leave the van running when you go into the homes. If you turn the van off it could freeze up and not start. The grocery store is the only place that has the electrical plugs for vehicles."

As I contemplated these things and realized I was about to continue this time-honored profession of quickly responding to a myriad of situations, I pulled up to the reservation. The elders greeted me warmly, and we conversed a bit about the culture of the Dene before getting down to business. I was grateful for the cultural lesson, considering I had just settled into this town.

I learned from them that the word Dene means "people" and they lived in many villages. They said I would be able to tell which village they were from by the bead design on their moccasins and the design on their parkas.

They also reaffirmed the thoughts I had on the way over-that respect is the key to living and working among these people.

"I hope you and your husband aren't avid hunters," one of the elders said, "because you won't be allowed to hunt (big game) here for the first two years. The Dene would see you as killing their environment and leaving nothing for their future. Hunting here is treated with the utmost respect. We believe all life is sacred and treat it as such. And we share everything with one another...clothing, fresh kills. We don't waste anything, and we keep only what we need in our homes. We don't have piles of clothing and refrigerators packed with leftovers the way your people do."

I could see he was very proud of what he was saying, proud of his heritage and his people.

"Also," began another, "the Dene tend to smoke and drink...But you would not be very well respected if one of the Dene saw you carrying a bottle of liquor that you'd bought at the store. They would assume you were a drunk, not that you were just going to have a drink with your family at dinner."

"And if you need to see the chief for any reason, his name is Chief Big Bear, and he is in a mobile home over there."

After my visit with the elders of the tribe, I went back to the hospital and was able to arrange the gerontology class for the nurses for the following day.

CHAPTER 5

EARLY EXPOSURE

He who has pity on the poor lends to the Lord, and
He will pay back what he has given.

(Proverbs 19:17)

I got my first taste of treating frostbite right out of the starting gate. Well, it didn't really surprise me considering I had been warned of how common it was here in the Northwest Territories. I wasn't prepared for the appearance of the most severe cases, however, until I actually saw one in the flesh... literally.

I remember arriving at one home in the morning. I left the van running because I wanted to make sure it would start once I had finished my visit. I didn't turn the heater on because I didn't want my feet and hands to sweat and then freeze up and cause frostbite-this happens very quickly.

The physical environment was quite interesting. The air was heavy with the smell of a fresh kill, with the blood of the piece of moose meat dripping all over the floor. The family had just received a fresh kill. Mr. Smallgeese, the man of the house, his foot wrapped in a well-worn dressing, was cutting the meat into steaks, no doubt, I thought, for the lunch and dinner meals that night.

His wife was in the living area making clothing from the skins of a moose and finishing up a pair of moccasins with beaver fur around the edge. The couple's two young toddlers were sleeping in a hammock nearby.

Sanitation had to be considered for this crucial situation. One of Mr. Smallgeese's feet was severely frostbitten. He would drink routinely and then wander outside in his bare feet. The alcohol numbed him to the cold.

When I unrolled the dressing off his foot, I not only got the full brunt of the putrid smell, his foot was brown to purplish blue and black. His one toe was barely attached. The amount of tissue death was so extensive that I knew his foot would need to be amputated.

"Mr. Smallgeese," I said, "I really need to get you to the hospital."

"No!" he replied emphatically. "You can't take me there. I will surely die there!"

"No, you won't," I assured him. "We just need to get you the treatment you need to get you better. I promise the medical staff will take good care of you and explain everything they're going to do."

As I continued to talk with Mr. Smallgeese, I was sure to let him know what to expect, what would potentially happen to him, being sure to recognize his fear. I don't attempt to cheer him by making light of the danger.

I put a dry, sterile dressings on his foot.

I could see some young Spruce tree shoots boiling on the stove. I had heard that the First Nations people use Spruce tree shoots and needles for promoting perspiration, reducing fevers. I was told that their healing system involved a connection with the natural environment as well as a spiritual element in the practice of the Medicine Man. They believed that only when harmony between nature and people were set right, could their health be restored. It was said that 80% of the First Nation people and the people who have lived here for some time, relied on traditional Medicine Man's rituals to meet their health care needs.

Herbal remedies, which the First Nation people have been using for thousands of years, stretch beyond the body's aches and pains and into the realm of spirituality and harmony. Herbs, plants, and even animal parts assist in cleansing the soul and bringing balance into the lives of the First Nation people and their environment, according to their tradition. They are used to heal colds, sore throats, and even gastrointestinal and musculoskeletal disorders.

Whole plants or sometimes parts of plants – the stem, roots, bark, leaves, or flowers – were used in creating a herbal remedy. These herbal remedies have been communicated from generation to generation as part of their oral traditions.

As I looked back at Mr. Smallgeese, I radioed the EMTs from the van, and they came dashing in with the stretcher. I looked for Mr. Smallgeese's coat. As I had seen many times before, his coat that was on a chair next to the wall, was actually frozen to the wall, due to the extreme cold.

The EMTs wrapped him up warmly with blankets from the ambulance. Then they put him in the back, and the four of us drove away.

We arrived at the hospital. A medical jet was arranged to travel from Edmonton to Hay River, for us to take him to the hospital there. It was difficult trying to hold onto the stretcher and crouch down to squeeze into that tiny medical jet. When we arrived in Edmonton, Mr. Smallgeese was to be checked in immediately. He had never been to a hospital in the south before, which was painfully obvious. We transferred him to a wheelchair, and I started to wheel him towards the elevator to take him up to his room. He looked increasingly frightened the closer he got to the opening of the elevator.

"What are you doing? What are you doing to me?"

"It's OK, Mr. Smallgeese," I said, trying to comfort him. "I'm just taking you to your room where you'll have a warm bed to lie in."

I then began to explain how an elevator worked and how safe it was to ride-that it was simply a lifting device.

I then remembered how I felt the first time we left Hay River to visit our family and friends in Ontario. We actually felt so out of place, like foreigners. We knew we looked different. We all needed haircuts, for one thing. Plus, we were wearing parkas made by an Inuit woman, so we looked like we lived in the extreme north. The crowds and noise of cars and people were almost foreign to us by now. Some people told us that if you stay too long in the North, you can't go back to that way of life. We left after two years.

On our way to Mr. Smallgeese's room, we saw another room with a group of First Nation people standing outside down the hallway. I quickly turned Mr. Smallgeese's wheelchair down another corridor. I knew what that meant – someone was dying. One of the First Nation women was making a pair of moccasins for the soon-to-be deceased. This hospital was for critically ill individuals. So not everyone who came here were cured, a sobering reminder every time I brought someone here.

We also passed an Inuit mom. She was carrying her baby in a pouch on her back. All of a sudden she leaned over, almost to the point you would think she was are getting ready to do a summersault. I gasped and held my breath as the baby flew out of the pouch. She caught the baby and continued to walk down the hall.

Once I took a young lady who had a high-risk pregnancy to the hospital and helped admit her. She had to have a C-section, but a beautiful new baby girl was born into the world to begin what would hopefully be a very long life. Babies are so life-affirming in a profession where we see so much illness and death.

John once took a man known as the town drunk to the hospital because he had throat cancer. John stayed with him throughout his chemotherapy treatment. John escorted him back to Hay River. He was terminal, so he died shortly after coming back

Back in Hay River, anytime I arrived for work in the hospital, I entered through the back door. If I saw a large wooden box out back, I knew someone had died. The box was the container the casket arrived in. Caskets were ordered from the hardware store. There was no funeral home so the casket was driven in the back of someone's truck to a place where the body would be held until the summer. The permafrost-frozen ground prevents any burials until the summer. Even in the summer, only the upper three feet or so, called the active layer, thaws.

Being a small-town environment, when there was a death, the town would shut down for the funeral because everyone knew everyone. It was a real tragedy when a beloved community member was gone.

The First Nation people had an interesting view of the afterlife, though, which gave them much hope and comfort. They believe ghosts remain earthbound and the dead retain a recognizable identity. They may even visit the living in dreams or visions. Each First Nation person's grave sites had a small open hut on top of it, which was filled with wood so the deceased person could keep warm in the winter.

I was awakened from my daydream by the doctor who informed us that indeed Mr. Smallgeese would need not only his toe amputated but his foot would have to be amputated. The doctor assured Mr. Smallgeese that he would most likely be fine. So I stayed with him a few days after his surgery and then flew back with him where we would need to keep a close eye on him and if necessary provide meals for him during his recovery.

CHAPTER 6

JANE

Pure and undefiled religion before God and the Father is this: to visit orphans and widows in their trouble, and to keep oneself unspotted from the world.

(James 1:27)

Our family had been attending church with the Dene Tribe on Sundays. Funny enough, the Dene people thought my husband was the pastor because he stood up front and led worship singing every Sunday. For the evening services, I would make a few dozen cookies; they would eat some and then put some in their pockets.

There was one woman, named Jane, who attended the church. She took care of babies born to teenage moms, as was the custom among the Dene people. She also suffered from Rheumatoid Arthritis. But despite the hardships with her health and the fact that she was advanced in age at this point, she had spent her life taking children into her home. She was a true heroine.

When Jane had an emergency, she would leave Carla one of the children she cared for, with us. That way, Eric had Jane's granddaughter to play with, who was only a year younger than Eric. Eric really liked Carla.

Every time he knew she would be coming over he would always say, "Oh wow! I get to see Carla!"

I had also formed a relationship with Carla, not just because of Eric, but because I picked her up every Sunday and took her to Sunday School. After church, Carla would join my family and spend the afternoon with us. I would prepare lunch, but Carla ate only when she was hungry, not necessarily when we sat down to eat. That was how things were done in her home.

Over time, our family had grown really close to Jane and Carla. I wanted to adopt Carla but didn't really know how to ask Jane about it.

That Monday, I went to Jane's home to administer her treatment for her Arthritis.

When I walked in, Jane was boiling something on the stove. As we began to talk, she shared with me that she was preparing something that would take care of her problems. Curious, I asked her what she was using and how she used the plants around the area for common conditions. That's what led to the conversation about how First Nation people believe that health is a continual process of staying strong spiritually, mentally, and physically. She said that they believe that keeping in harmony with those around them, their natural environment, and their creator would keep away illness and harm.

As Jane poured some hot spruce tea, I asked if I could sit at the table with her. As the two of us sat down and sipped tea together, I began to speak.

"Jane...you know that you and Carla are like family to us."

Jane nodded.

"I have something I really wanted to ask you. I just don't know how to do it."

"Just go ahead and ask child," she said, sipping her tea again while it was still hot.

"Well, you have done so much for the Dene community. I mean, I can't imagine the number of children you have cared for in your home over the years."

"I'm sure more than I can even remember at this point," she replied.

"Yeah...well..." I continued stammering, "I was just wondering if it would be possible for our family to adopt Carla."

There! I said it! Finally! I thought.

Jane looked at me a moment and smiled. Then she began her response.

"I'm sure that would be wonderful for your family. I know you all love her and I know that I'm not as young as I used to be. And I know she and Eric get along just like brother and sister."

Things seem to be looking good so far....

"But it is the custom of our people to take care of their own. So I'm afraid our customs would forbid such an adoption to take place. I'm so sorry."

A tear welled in my eye as I listened to her response, partly because I knew Carla would not be allowed to be a permanent part of our family, and partly because I knew I wouldn't be in Hay River forever, and there would come a time when we would not see Carla anymore.

Nonetheless, I told her, "I absolutely respect your tribe and your customs, so I understand completely."

"Thank you so much," she said. "And you can continue to bring Carla to church with you, and she can still play with Eric."

"I'm so glad," I responded.

It wasn't until about ten years ago I found out that my great, great grandmother was from the Cree tribe. We could have adopted Carla....

We finished our tea, and I asked her if I could examine Carla while I was there. Of course, she said, I could since I had done it so regularly. So I went to the bed where she was sleeping and woke her up.

I noticed lice on Carla's head, crawling through her hair.

"Uh oh," I said. "I don't think Eric and Carla will be playing together for a while after all. Carla has lice, and that's highly contagious. You'll need to keep her separate from other people for a while so they won't get it on them."

Then I went back to the van and pulled out some special shampoo that I carried with me, as lice was a common problem in Hay River. The shampoo needed to be used by everyone in the household and anyone who has been in close contact with Carla. Then I washed Carla's hair. I took the clothes she was wearing off her, took them and the bedding out to the van, and secured them in a bag that I would take to the special common area where I would wash the clothes.

Meanwhile, Jane went to get Carla some more clothes to put on her, and I left with the clothes to wash.

"Sorry I have to rush off, but I have to get started with this."

"Of course," Jane said.

CHAPTER 7

MEETING
THE CHIEF

Fear not, for I am with you; be not dismayed, for I am your God. I will strengthen you, yes, I will help you, I will uphold you with My righteous right hand.

(Isaiah 41:10)

One day I visited the home of Mr. Settingsun. It was my custom to look for smoke rising from a chimney. I didn't notice any smoke from his chimney. This was a troubling sign because it means that the wood stove is not burning wood. As I drove up to his home and prepared for the worst, my heart started to beat faster as I stepped out of the car.

I opened his door and said, "Mr. Settingsun" in a voice loud enough for him to hopefully hear me.

No answer.

I quietly began walking through his house and found him curled up in his bed in the corner of the room, with a pile of covers on top of him. I didn't know if he was dead or alive when I approached him. He was okay. But when I checked his refrigerator I found there was no food. There was also no wood outside his home for me to start a fire.

I have to do something, I thought to myself. He was obviously not going to eat anything right then. Nevertheless, I wondered how long it had been since he had eaten.

"Mr. Settingsun, don't you worry, OK? I'll be right back with some help."

I had previously observed where the Chief's office was located, so I got in the van and went to see him. His office was in a small trailer, and when I arrived, I saw a young lady sitting at the reception desk. So I asked if I could see the Chief regarding Mr. Settingsun. She escorted me to his office, which was right behind the reception area. I stood in the doorway and felt uncomfortable as my heart rate increased. The young lady guided me towards the Chief's desk where he was sitting.

As I began explaining Mr. Settingsun's dilemma to him, he just looked at me with no expression on his face. Fear came over me, as he stood and walked toward me. I'm only 5'2" tall, and he must have been about 6'8". I was terrified.

"Oh, no," I muttered.

"I'm Chief Big Bear."

I quietly snickered and so did he, breaking up the tension I was feeling because of Mr. Settingsun's condition and because of the Chief's massive size.

"Sounds like someone has been stealing from him. Unfortunately, we have a lot of discipline problems out here."

The Chief continued and said, "I remember one of my people telling me about a time when your husband helped out a Royal Canadian Mounted Police officer."

"Yes," I said, "that was the day when we were driving down the street, we saw a Royal Canadian Mounted Police officer struggling to get control and arrest three or four people who were drunk and fighting the officer."

I was thinking how, unlike major cities where there are lots of police backup, often the Royal Canadian Mounted Police officers in Hay River and other remote areas, stand alone in times of trouble.

I continued. "John stopped our car and got out to help. He was prepared to fight, if necessary. You see he has his Black Belt in karate and was a self-defense instructor for many years. The men from your tribe suddenly changed their entire attitude. What they did next took us by surprise. As John approached them, they stood up to shake his hand. John then asked them to do what the officer wanted. They got in the back of the officer's car."

"That is a good thing. It makes his job a lot easier as a correctional officer. Your husband has developed a lot of respect as a firefighter and EMT. I also know he is a spiritual leader in the church on my reservation..."

I began to think how John was considered a spiritual leader because of his involvement with the church on the reservation and how he would often stop and pray for people.

John led the singing at the church in the village where we worshiped together as a family. So they thought he was a pastor. It's important to note here, though, that First Nation people often do not judge "outsiders" by titles or initials, but by the way they conducted their lives. So, even though I was respected as a nurse, and John was recognized as a church leader, we were respected because we were well-thought-of, not because of our positions.

The Chief continued, "I think we need to go ahead and go to Mr. Settingsun's home. One of my assistants and I will follow you there."

When we arrived, we went inside, and the Chief spoke to Mr. Settingsun.

Then the Chief turned to me and said, "I know who did this. I know who stole his wood and food. I will take care of it."

The Chief instructed his aide where to retrieve Mr. Settingsun's wood.

CHAPTER 8

SHARING

But do not forget to do good and to share, for with
such sacrifices God is well pleased.

(Hebrews 13:16)

As I mentioned, the First Nation people shared everything with one another, including the animals killed during hunting trips. Sharing everything creates a sense of community; it bonds them with one another and with their culture. Never was this so apparent than when my son and I visited a nursing home. It was the first one in the area.

I still remember the very first, First Nation person we admitted to that nursing home. We had brand new clothes ready for him when he arrived. But he said he only needed one pair of pants, a shirt, a pair of socks, one pair of shoes and no pajamas. He said that if he had too much, it would weigh his spirit down when he died. This tribe had in the past lead such a nomadic lifestyle that even at this time he felt anything extra would weigh him down, right into eternity.

I also remember the time a First Nation woman made me a pair of moccasins. I asked her to fill in the top of the moccasins with beads. She said according to their beliefs too many beads would weigh me down and my spirit would not be able to go to heaven. I was reminded that earthly things could weigh us down if they take the place of our Lord Jesus Christ.

Anyway, as Eric and I walked into the nursing home, the residents were sitting in a circle, preparing to do an activity. As Eric and I joined the circle, I was wondering what kind of arts and crats were planned for that day. As I was thinking about this, behind me arrived a couple of very tall First Nation men, carrying sacks.

They walked to the middle of the circle, dropped the sacks, and started to empty them. They were full of dead rabbits.

I froze. I didn't know how this was going to affect my son. I remember how sad he was when he had to leave his pet bunny behind when we left our old home for Hay River. I still remember consoling him on the plane.

The men were preparing to skin the rabbits. One man leaned over to Eric and started to show him how to properly skin a rabbit so it would be one piece.

I tried not to react, but I was holding my breath, waiting for a response from Eric while the people around him acted as if this was a regular activity.

As the man held the rabbit down where Eric could see it, Eric reached out and started touching the rabbit's fur, petting it curiously. Then he looked up and saw the knife in the man's other hand; he was holding it away from Eric to avoid a dangerous situation. Eric reached out for the knife, even though the man wasn't going to give it to him. If he had been a First Nation child, though, he probably would have let Eric try it.

"Your boy is a born hunter," the man said. "We could teach him the skill of the hunt."

"I deeply appreciate the offer; he's just a little young for that, I think."

"Oh, we learn to hunt when we are children. In fact, there is a game children play where they slide a spear across the ice. It teaches them how to slide it straight across the ground at an animal they are aiming at that is lying on the ice."

"Thank you so much once again," I reiterated. "I just think he's a little too young now. Perhaps in a couple more years."

I was so relieved this turned out the way it did.

The man gave each of the residents a rabbit to skin, and they all enjoyed the activity together, even Eric.

CHAPTER 9

CHRISTMAS IN HAY RIVER

Glory to God in the highest, And on earth peace, goodwill toward men!

(Luke 2:14)

Christmas is a time of rest, reflection, and recuperation from the year's events while looking forward to what the next year brings. This is especially true as a nurse. Considering I have seen so much illness and so many tragedies throughout the years, focusing on Jesus coming to earth to save us holds a special beauty for me. This special time of year takes my focus off this earth and puts it on Christ.

At times, however, the mechanics of celebrating Christmas was a bit challenging in Hay River. I remember one Christmas where I was baking with limited supplies because the grocery store ran out of chocolate chips, nuts, raisins, and cherries, and the next shipments were not expected to arrive until January.

I was not only preparing to do some Christmas baking but also was baking a cake for one of the seniors, who was turning ninety years old. Although she was not a First Nation person, she had lived in Hay River since her early twenties. This lady was born before her time. She had planted the first vegetable garden here in Hay River and had lived on her own since her husband died fifty years ago. When I would visit her, she would share many stories about her hardships but always with humor.

I remember visiting her every Thursday. She would pull out a couple of mugs from her cabinet and say:

"Let's sit down and talk. I just made a fresh pot of coffee yesterday."

It was very common for someone to offer you coffee that had been sitting on the stove for some time. The coffee would be thick and strong. Depending on who you visited, they may offer you coffee that was made by boiling a pot of water on the stove and then throwing in some coffee grounds. Now that coffee was a challenge to drink, with all those coffee grounds.

Meanwhile, John and Eric had gone to the woods to get a Christmas tree-it was the only place we could get one. Driving down the road, in minus fifty degrees Fahrenheit weather, John spotted a beautiful tree, probably the only nice-looking tree in Hay River. He got out of the truck with his axe and stepped out into the snow to go cut it down.

Where he walked the snow was so deep it was almost up to his neck. But like a real trooper, he plowed through and placed the axe on the trunk of the tree. One hit and the tree cracked and fell. Unfortunately, most of the needles fell off with it because of the extreme cold.

John knew he couldn't drag it back to the truck, so he held it upright and walked it through the neck-deep snow and placed it gently in the back, of the truck, hoping to preserve the rest of the pine needles. But as John and Eric rode home with the tree, the truck rocked from side to side because the roads were what we called-wash board roads, not exactly paved. Due to the frigged weather, by the time John walked into our home with the tree, it had lost about three-fourths of its needles.

When I saw this poor, decaying excuse for a tree, I said, "This isn't our Christmas tree, is it?"

"Yep, here it is," John said. "Isn't it a beauty?" he said with a smile, trying not to bust out laughing at our Charlie Brown Christmas tree.

I had gotten the decorations out while they were gone in anticipation of putting them on a magnificent tree. Even still, after we hung the decorations on it (Eric, of course, helped decorate the bottom limbs, as that was all he could reach), and adorned it with lights, I was reminded of Jesus as the light of the world. It truly was decorated with God's beauty.

The next morning, I finished preparing our Christmas dinner, despite the fact that we didn't have all the ingredients from the store to make the dinner I had envisioned. But that didn't matter. John read from Matthew 1:22-23, citing the prophecy in Isaiah, "The virgin will conceive and give birth to a son, and they will call him Immanuel' (which means 'God with us')."

I had been witnessing and learning beautiful things during my stay in Hay River, which lasted until 1991, a fact I reflected on that particular Christmas. I had learned to "Rejoice always, pray continually, give thanks in all circumstances; for this is God's will for you in Christ Jesus," (1 Thessalonians 5:16-18).

We ate at noon because the sun was still up. Eric reached for his long johns, ski pants, sweater, silver fox-lined parka, duffle-lined mittens, duffle-lined boots, and his scarf. He was now ready. John got dressed and called for Sheba as he took Eric outside for a ride on the sled. It was a beautiful Northwest Territories Christmas....

NOTES

NOTES

NOTES

NOTES

NOTES

NOTES

NOTES

NOTES

NOTES

NOTES

NOTES

NOTES

NOTES

NOTES

NOTES

NOTES

NOTES

NOTES

NOTES

NOTES

NOTES

NOTES

NOTES

NOTES

Printed in the United States
By Bookmasters